CONNECTIONS 8

Poetry and Mus  **f**

KRCB FM

JAXON'S
PRESS

This Anthology of Poems
is Published by

Jaxon's Press
P.O. Box 2774
Santa Rosa, CA 95405
jaxonspress@gmail.com

Cover: "The Dinner Party" by Sterling Hoffman
Used by permission.
Photograph of cover painting by Kathleen McCallum

Editors: Alison Jacobs Maldonado, Sarah Estalee Baker

Photographs by permission of their owners:

Cynthia Helen Beecher
Guy Biederman
Elizabeth Herron
Sarah Estalee Baker
Guy Biederman

A portion of publishers' royalties will be donated to KRCB FM.
Northern California Public Media.

ISBN 978-1-7378349-4-6

Acknowledgements

Without Doug Jayne listening to his audience, and for the willingness and extraordinary abilities of the KRCB staff, this collection of poetry and its accompanying recordings, the CD of its poems, some accompanied by various original musical tracks, would not have been published.

Gratitude to Sterling Hoffman for his permission to use his painting for cover art. Thank you, also, to Kathleen McCallum for donating her photograph.

Thanks to the Jaxon's Press team for their stick-to-itiveness and due diligence down the wire to the book's public release.

CONNECTIONS 8
Poetry and Music in Benefit of
KRCB FM

With a pale light, I journeyed round the hall
And found a door deep sunken in the wall,
The least of doors; beyond on a dim plain . . .

William Butler Yeats[i]

Contents

Introduction

This collection of poems is an intimate anthology from 17 poets residing in Northern California from San Francisco to Mendocino County, and further still to Cape Cod, Massachusetts. These artists delve into sought-after coastlines, mountains, and rivers, listening deeply, as they ride roads through forests, to immerse and observe. They unearth and illustrate rare, transcendent, and sometimes gut-wrenching moments as we read and hear their rhythms and phrases.

Since the earliest days of artists reciting poems and playing instruments, KRCB has been a unique part of radio life. KRCB is an innovator; it creates a public listening environment where poetry and music are recognized as their own art form. A listener might hear Jack Kerouac reading October in the Railroad Earth accompanied by the silky piano stylings of Steve Allen, or any poet in this book, or from neighboring Sonoma, our National Poet Laureate, Ada Limón.

My first experience listening to artists reciting poetry with music on the radio was Pierrette Montroy's *Inkwell*. The interviews and performances she held were beamed live from a trailer at the back lot, hunched in the shadow of a baseball stadium where the Sonoma County Crushers made their debut in 1995.

Through the years, KRCB has been the microphone for a myriad of significant topics, and it continues to be a mainstay for voices that speak and sing, read and recite, and listen to poetry with a musical underscore swirling along in its presence. The Station's interviews and conversations continue to foster the freedom to cross-pollinate and become part of a beloved community revered by its dedicated artists and listeners.

Drought
Spring in December

Timothy Williams

Star clouds cascade over the old mountain home
Fire hums, flue's crackling, my back's against the flame
Today is a spring day in December
planting daffodils at the finale of the low sun
Not a drop of rain has fallen this fall
yet a few fell a while ago -- without a sound

No, it's a worry of a thought these about drought
though I must say, we still float in hot mineral waters
There are cold creeks and hot springs on the rugged hill
this Lake County Ponderosa, Oak, Bay and Fir studded range
There'll be a day of dread this summer
if we don't get any rain

The counties of California brace for the freeze
Another morn' of frost and sun
without a lonely cloud, day after day
yet I cannot help but wonder why
it is spring in December

I'll plant a bed of daffodils by your garden windmill
as these days I see the yellowest light,
splinter in the golden sun that warms
the already sweltering earth
without a worry of a time, by and by, of a drought

As I see it, it wouldn't hurt
to pray or dance or dream of rainstorms
and moods brought to life by the power of a dream

And that would be that you and I would run
through the wildest and wettest of rainstorms in California history
filling the lakes, wells, streams, reservoirs, kitchen sinks
and, yeah, swimming pools

I wouldn't mind a cloudy day
where the world shakes the change we hope for
Tomorrow, I long to hear the Dry Creek singing never end
and the sky growing dark with thunder calling

As I see it, it wouldn't hurt
to pray or dance or dream of rainstorms
and moods brought to life by the power of a dream
of rain

The Desert

Jackson Ahern

There is more pain in the desert
Than the imaginations of a thousand poets.
There is more beauty in the desert
Than the smiles of a thousand brown eyed children.
There is less water in the desert
Than a cruel man has tears.
More stars in the desert night
Than grains of sand beneath your thirsty boots.
You may hold it for a lifetime,
But never own it.
Just when you think you know it
It will change its shape.
When you call out
It will change its name:
Sahara, Gobi, Mojave, Kalahari, Arabian, Patagonian.
From the Great Basin sagebrush
To the mountains of Eliat,
If you look twice it will own you!
If you try to forget
The Joshua tree will haunt your dreams.
If you try to run
The Cholla cactus will jump and grab you.
When you are too dry to speak
The ruby fruit of the prickly pear
Will touch your tongue.
It will honor the bold
And punish the fool!
Remember to carry water,
A lot of water!

dare, dare not

Cynthia Helen Beecher

a. n. beecher is elected by a slam
mayor 1850s ohio
abolitionist evangelistic pacifist oberlin
elm trees compete for sky and admiration along the avenue

a. n. beecher writes lively loving letters
to his children pioneering out west to his
shirttail relatives back east the dour the ribald the betters
boys in short pants play stickball along the avenue

a. n. beecher tends his wife with kindliness kisses swift furtive
gardens in the season corn beans peas potatoes for the table
flowers for her strawberries and watermelons for him
farm carts work horses donkeys ash peddlers labor along the
avenue

a. n. beecher welcomes neighbors and politicians
pressed around the fire they seek his counsel
read his periodicals sip his sweet tea nestle among his ideas
laughter and sleigh bells ring out up and down the avenue

a. n. beecher grows a house full of plants to liven the breath
feathers strange bones shells rocks western ocean sand
years of daily journals entreaties for right and good
line the pathways of his rooms there above the avenue

a. n. beecher takes his walks eats apples and vegetables
makes popcorn balls for sale whistles his tunes builds greenhouses
and birdhouses tips his hat to those ladies traipsing up and down
the avenue

a. n. beecher holds the town secret discreet in his journal
  three brown guests at dinner they are not yet safe or free
  seek shelter from the dogs the heat of malarial fevers whistling whips
  their songs dare not rise dare not sweeten the air along the avenue

Night of The Floating Groove

Guy Biederman

Poetry on a barge at high tide.
Poets sharing, people nodding, adding polite applause.
Mamadou on drum made no move to play, one foot tapping.

After the last poet read, last chapbook sold, potluck began—
pizzas, pies, salads, and cheese, somebody brought frijoles. Crowd
feathered out.

Lynnae asked Mamadou if he wouldn't play one,
Vincent brought his djembe from the car.
Night kicked into beat after that and the humming toadfish
on the floating hull synched underneath it all.

Poet followed poet, sounds followed sound.
Stage fright Singer held the mic, her nails glowing colors,
sang a song from lines she'd heard, finding her voice and words.

Laureates knocked.
Whitman peeked through the window.
Emily texted from an Uber, maybe tried to facetime.
Sinbad rowed to get her. And things weren't the same after that—
beat, words, drums twined
as braids of line called joy. We floated, we jammed,
we grooved to this pulse called life.

This morning I awoke hung over but hadn't had a drink.
Barge immaculate. Had the evening happened. Did it matter.
Phone rang, someone trying to facetime. On the counter,
a ribbon wrapped around daisies, tulips, and roses
from a garden I didn't own.

January- Moon of the Wolf, the Hunger Moon
(An Excerpt from *Last Report*)

Elizabeth Herron

Low of 19 degrees.
The long bones of cold settle into evening
as geese settle on the marsh, wings tucked,
feathers fluffed.

A low pressure trough hauls rain
from Alaska all the way to *oona pa'is*
where Coyote overturned his boat
and spilled the springs, creeks, river,
and called the salmon home.

The lovers turn in sleep -- face to face,
breath to breath, back to back.
Warm under quilts they fit
like sections of citrus – hips, thighs, salty sweet.

Migrating north, the gray whales
stitch air to ocean under THE heavy rain
that heaves in along the coast and across the valley
to the Sierras, dusting the foothills with snow,
deeper on the upper slopes closing the roads.

Knotted winds. Tangle
of the lovers' hair, hands, salty sweet.

February- Moon of the Long Snow
(An Excerpt from *Last Report*)

Through a flutter of snow in the high country,
the wolverine shuffles hundreds of miles
to the edge of extinction.

Stars hum all night over cliffs
of granite and glaucophane, hum

over the dead whale on Bolinas Beach
whose eye had seen their light from mid-ocean,
who had known the gravitational paths
of planets.

Fast clouds travel the darkness
over the hips, thighs, the salty-sweet
dreams of the lovers.

When did love and death align?
How did life's meaning marry its grief?

Rain gusts over the house
where the lovers sleep. Breath and silence
hold them.

March- the Worm Moon
(An Excerpt from *Last Report*)

Before new buds, a last dry leaf,
tugs away from the oak
and floats on a wet wind high
over the town.

Let the wind unwind
toward the rebirth of stars, back
to the heart of all origins.

Let the wind take me
with the last leaf torn west. Let me rise
from the bones of whale and wolverine

as the marsh ghosts rise in the chill of dusk.
Let me rise with them.

Let me leave behind
the world of salt and sorrow.

Let me rise
from the body of what I have loved.

Last Port of Call
(An Excerpt from *The Thief of Yellow Roses*)

Jonah Raskin

At noon on the Barbary Coast
on the last day of the year,
the sky turns a true blue above
you,
the tattooed sailor, with
pierced earlobes who sails the
seven seas in storms and becalmed in
doldrums where you long
for the love you lost in your
last port of call.

Crossing Borders
(An Excerpt from *The Thief of Yellow Roses*)

Sailor,
you walk with her on the
beach, not as often as you'd
like, so you walk alone,
hover where water meets land,
gaze at the space where she
once stood, remember that
she offered you her hand to
steady your unsteady sea legs.

The Holiest of Harbors
(An Excerpt from *The Thief of Yellow Roses*)

You arrive at the end
of your voyage in the
holiest of harbors
where you secure sails,
stow gear, amble down
gangplank, steady
sea legs and
kiss the parched earth
beneath bare feet.

Gee Wizdom

Pierrette Montroy

I've been livin' next door to my own life
I've been sittin' in the last row at the church of my existence
I've been a spectator of fear in a prison of my own history
I've been a murderer to all things possible
And some kinda tattletale on myself

I've been sittin' back from the corners of my own eyes
Not wantin' to get too close to the lights
I've been real small,
only stretched out to look big from that moment to this
Grown up but inside, small

I've been wantin' to say something, do something, be something
But I was waitin' for them to notice me back there in the last pew
Starin' up at people's overcoats and Sunday hats
Waitin' for communion

But now findin' out suddenly that communion is me, her,
that one who's been waitin'
Gee Wiz! Everything is comin' into focus now
Just like a new pair a' glasses
Spectacles of the gods!

You know I'd pitched a tent along beside that body
Like it was some kinda monument
A natural wonder having nothing to do with me
A place to visit from time to time but not mine
Men roused her from her sleep
and brought her home to ecstasy some nights

But you'd be waitin' for that one
Livin' next door to your own life

A word I did not want to hear was this one sorry word
Alone
Seemed like someone oughta have been there
A Guardian Angel maybe, or a man
Helping me and making sure I wasn't lonely
But now findin' out suddenly that Gabriel blows
his horn and says,
You are alone, my fallen friend, and where I lead
there, no one but you can follow.
And I shake my fist at him and say,
If I am so alone, then what are you doin' here?
No, big Angel, you won't be leadin' me just yet,
I've got some mighty celebratin' left to do and anyway
Everything is comin' into focus now
Just like a new pair a' glasses
Haven't you noticed it?
The goddess, she wears spectacles!

So I declare a pilgrimage to my own life
The holy places where kingdom came
Whether States of these United
or States of Grace
I hoist my rucksack
and set my pace

Down Around the Embarcadero

Jack Crimmins

I'm not going I'm not staying
I'm selling my poems
on the corner in my
railroad cap typing out
dreams down around
Fisherman's Wharf
down around
the Embarcadero
every so often
5 bucks a poem
do you see me I see you
the tourists buy my poems
as rough-edged souvenirs
now don't be telling lies
I'm tempted to disappear
east of Santa Fe and
west of nowhere
but I've got a rent controlled
place south of an alley
in Glen Park, San Francisco
I found a bookstore
in the Mission that'll
carry my books for sale
it's morning it's evening
somewhere it's late afternoon
poems for 5 bucks

I've got poems for
a thousand bucks too
you get what you pay for
yet it's all spirit and heart
with a serious nod to
Black Mountain poets
to the Beats and
SF Renaissance poets
if I can just find my way
to the end of the page
the end of the poem
Don Ewell is playing
boogie woogie piano
a Jelly Roll Morton jazz tune
it's early it's late they
changed the time again
I'm living quiet and easy
worked hard through
and through so
this poem's for my brothers
for my sister and for you
catch me down at the Marina
right near North Beach
out in the Avenues
I'm lost I'm gone
distance intimacy
poetry as truth

The Road

Gwynn O'Gara

I am the road.
You drive on me, over me.
You're always on top of me
then rolling along.

One road's the same as another to me.
I love my car. I need to move, go,
leave. You're always staying.
You can't help it. You're a road.
I'm pointy and hard and fast. I go.
You're a road bed. I can rest in you
or zoom over you.

I am the road.
You drive on me, over me.
You're always on top of me
then rolling along.

I'll lead you to a dead end
get you stuck in the mud.
You'll have to get out and walk
put your feet all over me, feel me
with your soles, touch me.

You'll go slow, discovering each inch of me
grateful I'm between you and the dirt,
protecting you from what came before us,
what surrounds us, what we cannot enter.

Falling

Larry Robinson

In these awe-filled days of fire and flood and plague
We watch and wait and wonder
When that fierce hand
Might reach at last for us.

Those of us not yet touched by calamity
Quake, knowing in our bones
That though we may be spared
This time, time will level us all.

No magic amulets, no prayers, no masks,
Good deeds or good looks
Can promise protection
From our terminal human condition.

And those who have watched a child
Swept forever from our arms
Or fled the flames that swallowed
Our hopes and our memories

Or hid from the bombs or the virus
Or the predator's gaze
Know that nothing now will ever be the same -
As if anything ever were.

For all of us are falling
Like ashes, like rain,
Like petals, like leaves;
But we all are falling together.

And if we knew, in truth,
There was nowhere to land,
Tell me: could we know the difference
Between falling and flying?

Coltrane

Ed Coletti (for David Bromige)

ever changing
trane

morphing
trane
what chrysalis?
trane
what vehicle
brought you here?
trane
spiritual in D
trane
night train
A train
right train
trane
take the light train
trane
outta sight
trane
no cliché for you
trane
outta sight
is where you dwell
trane
you created
outta sight
trane
weaver's sax
that's you
trane

sax and you
so blue
trane
blue and you
soul and body
together you
trane
magic man too
few knew
trane
you heal this world
trane
keep on keepin' on with <u>that</u>
trane
no world a turd's worth
without you
trane

thank you
thank you
thank you
trane
thank you for the ocean too
trane, your slow deliberate sea
trane
trane, just the ocean you and me
trane, bluest blue sea you and me
trane, receive communion
me and you man, now and forever
you and me and that crazy piano
for two trane now and forever

one trane, earth is still
trane
bass bass so blue trane
with that molasses piano so crazy
blue trane, and you that sax
so mellow blue trane
what can I do, trane?

they say you are gone trane
crazy and gone trane
your soul and your brain,
trane mellow insane, trane
now bass is bowing, trane
oceans keep flowing, trane
bass, keyboard, sax all blowing
trane, you just keep going,
trane, you just keep blowing
and showing me you're still glowing
trane now and forever
keep feeding and seeding
bleeding indeeding not leaving
this world without you to cease
turning while those who heard you
would wonder wander and wonder
again where are you so much one,
where have you gone?
and only the music, the everything
will answer only

here , man, the gift
here, man, the joy
right here man
right here man
right here
this only moment
right here right now
man!

The Request

Mary Kane

My father had a collection of teeth -
Mr. Ramos's teeth and Mrs. O'Riordan's. Agatha
Jones's and Lillian
whose last name I never knew. And my Uncle
Henry's and Aunt Helena's. He kept them
in a clay bowl
on a shelf by the kitchen window
and sometimes he'd pick up a handful
and stand there in the sunlight,
eyes closed, his whole body stilled
like he was divining histories and futures
in the tiny weights of what he held. Once,
I saw him shake the teeth
until they made of his hand
a loose rattle. Then he
spilled them on the table and asked me
to tell him a story. Which I did.
Because how can you say no to someone
with a heart like that.

Eva in the key of D

Jim Morgan

My dissertation advisor once asked me
if I could go back in time
who would I choose to meet,
and I was well down a leaf-strewn lane
filled with birds, beasts, and flowers
before considering London in 1599
to hear Shakespeare beneath the boards cry "Sign!"
or perhaps 8th-century BCE Greece
to find Homer, or whoever wrote down
from memory Odysseus's wanderings,
and see if the poet was blind and played the lyre,
or 1308 in Florence to discuss with Dante
the nine circles of eternal pain and suffering.

If the trip is one-way
and there's no coming back,
I'm not traveling beyond the realm
of modern dentistry, though I
could find Frost, Stevens, Williams, and Eliot,
Joyce, Rilke, Faulkner, and Beckett,
Neruda, Bishop, and Plath,
or catch Satchmo, Byrd, Monk, or Miles,
Dylan playing Gerde's Folk City
and The Beatles in Hamburg where,
Lennon said, they were at their best—

though if I could choose just one,
I would be in D.C. in the early 90s,
at Pearl's and Blues Alley when Eva
sings "Somewhere Over the Rainbow."
I'd send her a scotch and milk
or whatever she drinks,
audiences so spare and silent
she asks between songs,
Is anyone awake?

Afterwards, I'd offer to carry her guitar
or groceries or whatever,
heck, ask her to marry me
just to lie down beside that voice.

Having better guitar players to choose from,
she'd refuse, though I'd still be at The Bayou
that last night in '96, people getting ready
to be taken to the river and over troubled waters,
dancing time after time and cheek to cheek
with her family and friends when the songbird
closes on "What a Wonderful World,"
autumn leaves filling fields of gold,
melanoma burrowing in her bones.

River Road
For Chuck Torliatt

Bill Vartnaw

We are driving on River Road
Actually Chuck is driving
& I'm riding shotgun
in his cherried-out classic
I don't know what it is
I'm not into cars that way
but it's cool
& he's been working on it
since he was in high school
& since I graduated this year
That's been at least two years
& he's got it just the way he wants it

We are driving on River Road
above the Russian River
& between the redwoods
& Chuck says, "You want to see
my overdrive!"
& I say, "Yea!" because I know
he wants to show it to me
though I don't know what it is
& Chuck steps on it
& we're going pretty fast
& then he pulls a lever
& our heads kick back
& I laugh
& he laughs

& our parents are back at Armstrong Woods
Celebrating a birthday
or an anniversary
& we are hanging out for the first time
Driving on River Road
I look down to see
The ferry boat that runs
From Rio Nido to Guerneville
Back & forth, back & forth
Maybe a half dozen times each day
A summer tradition that my family took each year
When I was a kid
That boat played Bobby Darin's "Splish Splash"
over its loud speaker the first year
But then changed to Doris Day singing
"*Que sera, sera*
Whatever will be, will be"
Over & over & over again
Trying to create this idyllic moment
When you know the song came
From an Alfred Hitchcock movie
Where things really weren't as they seemed

You might expect
dangerous rapids around the bend
Or that the river was polluted
& was impossible to swim in without getting sick or dying
But this was California in 1967...
The next day Chuck would put his car

"up on blocks" & get ready
To report to basic training
In the fall I would go college
Where I began to march against the war
I didn't see Chuck again
28 years later, I found his name
On the wall in Washington D.C.
I scratched it into one of my notebooks
Hoping one day I would write
this poem
Without anger
About driving on River Road

Because it was such a gift

Chaoite

Melissa Eleftherion

Dark grey mass

Shock-metamorphosed

From meteorite

You abrade

Easily

Scale off memory of impact —

        Your shell

        Not so hard it crumbles

        Not so vulnerable it shatters

Resilience   a specimen of the long game

Polymorphous – a learned behavior for trauma

Crystals have such nice faces

In a family of diamonds

Sub-metallic lustre

Your allotropic

Double consciousness

White carbon

Thin bones

Between This Town and the Next

Jim Cohn

I know how a gaping hole
Swallows up all fear
It takes away all you've overcome
And all that you hold near
And sometimes when you think
It's taken all your best
You find it on the long way
Between this town and the next

All along the river bank
Sweet as doubt and faith
Crickets keeping perfect time
With all that silence grace
The open path in front of you
It exits up ahead
Somewhere between
This town and the a next

Take a letter to Maria
Tell her I miss her every day
I see her incense eyes
And all that's lost and gained
And all around me walls rise and fall
That never did exist
Where's everybody anyway
Between this town and the next

I take it where I find it
Dream dreams I'll never see
Messengers speak of the forgiveness
Wherever you may be
I've been beyond the sunset
And the sunset don't regret
The long way between this town
and the next

Doe

Georgina Marie Guardado

I never really expected to forgive myself
for killing an animal in the dark of night.

Rather, I expected to one day receive forgiveness
from the buck himself, whose face I saw
as if it were magnified
when my vehicle suddenly struck him,
the loud sound of metal shrinking into itself.

A bright white light ingrained in my memory
as if the moon came bursting down
in an effort to save him from the catastrophe
of what it is to be a human.

 Invading the quiet interrupting grace

Yes, another deer poem is in the making
because across the way is a doe standing in drought
reaching her tongue up to tree leaves.

 I want to be rid of confessions

Each step she takes, rings expand across the murky body of water
exposing oak roots and hidden stones

 I want to exist without guilt

 I want to be her

A woman said to me, *your eye sees the beauty*
and I want to ask, why does it also see so much sorrow?
her sun-yellow afghan challenging me to find only joy.

The doe is seeking refuge from the heat now
entangled in thin branches and ankle-deep water.
So much depends upon the quiet she carries with her
how it reaches out to me
I try my best not to make a sound.

Author Biographies
(in Order of Appearance)

Timothy Williams has been writing since the 1960s, and his first chapbook, *Sleepless Fires,* was published by Running Wolf Press in Healdsburg, CA. He began Poetry Band with guitarist Kevin Haapala, bassist Sam Page, and drummer Don Connolly. In 2003, they recorded *Lunch at Lolas*, an album of poetry and music. Timothy started Jaxon's Press to support his publishing passions. He resides in Sonoma and Lake Counties with his wife—a teacher, songwriter, and musician— Sarah Baker.

Jackson Ahern grew up in the traditional Yankee culture of the Northeast in Pennsylvania and New Hampshire, but his adult life was spent in the western culture of Arizona, Idaho, and California. His literary influences are everything from Robert Frost to Cowboy Poetry. Being a professional musician for fifty years led him to love song lyrics, especially those of Bob Dylan and Joni Mitchell. He writes everything from science fiction to children's stories.

Cynthia Helen Beecher, a descendant of pioneers, grew up watching and listening. She lived for nine years in central and southern Africa and is at work on a collection of poetry and linked short stories set there. She is a published photographer, poet, and writer. She is the author of the *"Send Me No Ants"* chapbook and the textbook, *The Rainmaker's Dog*. A.N. Beecher is her maternal great-great grandfather.

Guy Biederman is the author of *Translated From The Original*, one-inch punch fiction, and *Nova Nights*, poetry, both from Black Lawrence Press, as well as four other books of prose and poetry. His work has appeared in many journals including *Carve, Bull, MacQueen's Quinterly,* and *The San Franciscan,* and will also be published in *Best Micro Fictions* in 2024. A former peace corps volunteer and creative writing college instructor, Guy lives with his wife Phyllis on a houseboat in Sausalito and walks the planks daily.

Elizabeth Herron is author of *Insistent Grace* and most *recently In the Cities of Sleep* (both from Fernwood Press), as well as *The Poet's House; Desire Being Full of Distances*; and five chapbooks. Elizabeth C. Herron's writing has appeared in *Reflections; West Marin Review; Free State Review; Comstock Review; Fire and Rain, Ecopoetry of California; Parabola; Face to Face: Women Writing on Faith, Mysticism* and *Awakening;* and *What Kind of Ancestor Do You Want to Be.* The Mesa Refuge for Writers, the NEA, and the Foundation for Deep Ecology have supported her work. She is a Fellow of the International League of Conservation Writers and the Poet Laureate of Sonoma County (2022 to 2024).

Jonah Raskin wrote verse before he arrived in Sonoma County, but he didn't begin to think of himself as a poet until he lived in West County for more than a decade, joined a writing group, and performed his work with other poets in Graton, Healdsburg, Santa Rosa, Cotati, and live on KRCB.

Pierrette Montroy is a life-long writer, poet, and performer who has hosted three public radio shows over the years at KVMR, KRCB and Radio Ariège. Her original live poetry shows include *Gratitudes* and *Real Men Write Poems*. Today, Pierrette enjoys working with young people, beginning with her own nine grandchildren.

Jack Crimmins is the author of *Kit Fox Blues*, with an introduction by Diane di Prima; *The Rust Life*; *Dancing In The Sun Room;* and his latest book, *The Edge of Rain*. He has worked for many years as a licensed psychotherapist and lives in Santa Rosa, CA.

Gwynn O'Gara served as Sonoma County Poet Laureate 2010-2012 and taught with California Poets in the Schools for twenty-five years. Her latest book is *We Who Dream* from Finishing Line press. Her husband, the pianist Rob Catterton, composed the song "*Another Dream.*"

Larry Robinson is a retired psychotherapist, recovering politician, and practicing potter. He is the founder and producer of Rumi's Caravan, a performance ensemble dedicated to restoring the soul of the world through reviving the oral tradition of poetry. He lives in Sebastopol with his wife Cynthia Kishi.

Ed Coletti. Internationally published Sonoma County poet, founded and hosts the thrice-annual Poetry Festival at Cafe Frida Gallery in Santa Rosa. Ed's tribute poem "Coltrane" (for David Bromige) is from his music-based collection *Apollo Blue's Harp*. Following the loss of their Fountaingrove home to the 2017 Tubbs Fire, Ed and Joyce Coletti relocated successfully to Downtown Santa Rosa.

Mary Kane's recent collection of tiny stories is titled *In the Book I'm Reading* (One Bird Books, 2023). Her poetry and stories have appeared in numerous journals, including *Beloit Poetry Journal, FRiGG, Smokelong Quarterly, and Poetry Daily*. She is the author of several chapbooks and one full-length poetry collection, *Door* (One Bird Books, 2015). She lives on Cape Cod where she walks, reads, makes envelopes, teaches, writes, and engages in creative collaborations.

Jim Morgan grew up in Silver Lake, Ohio, received a BA in English from Case Western Reserve University, an MA in Creative Writing: Poetry from Boston University—where he studied with Anne Sexton, George Starbuck, and John Malcolm Brinnin—and an MA and a Ph.D. in English Literature from Tufts University. He has published three books of poetry: *Harlequin's Guitar: A Fable in 67 Improbable Improvisations*, *Procession of Souls*, and *Crows*. A retired professor in the Humanities Department at Massachusetts Maritime Academy, he is a member of Cape Coda, a classic rock band. He and his wife live with two cats on Cape Cod.

Bill Vartnaw was the seventh Poet Laureate of Sonoma County, serving 2012-2013. He established Taurean Horn Press, an independent poetry press, in 1974 in San Francisco and moved it to Sonoma County in 1998. He is the present director of the Petaluma Poetry Walk, a day-long poetry festival on the third Sunday in September celebrated at various venues in downtown Petaluma.

Melissa Eleftherion (she/they) is a writer, a librarian, and a visual artist. Born and raised in Brooklyn, she is the author of *field guide to autobiography*, *gutter rainbows*, and 12 chapbooks from various presses. Melissa currently lives in Northern California where she manages the Ukiah Branch Library, curates the LOBA Reading Series, and serves as Ukiah Poet Laureate Emeritus. Recent work is available at www.apoetlibrarian.wordpress.com.

Jim Cohn, poet, spoken word artist, editor, publisher, and curator, studied with American poets Allen Ginsberg and Anne Waldman at the Jack Kerouac School of Disembodied Poetics in Boulder, Colorado. He is the founder of the online Museum of American Poetics (poetspath.com). The author of 12 books of poetry and poetics and 8 recordings, Cohn published *Treasures for Heaven: Collected Poems 1976-2021* in 2022.

Georgina Marie Guardado is the 2020-2024 Poet Laureate of Lake County, CA, and a Poets Laureate Fellow with The Academy of American Poets. She is the Literacy Program Coordinator for the Lake County Library, President of the Mendocino Coast Writers' Conference, and a graduate student and scholar of the Kwame Dawes Mapmakers and Master of Fine Arts Merit endowments at the Pacific University MFA in Writing program. Her work has appeared in Poets.org, Humble Pie Magazine, Gulf Coast Journal, Yellow Medicine Review, The Muleskinner Journal, and more.

Publisher Notes

Also by Jaxon's Press
Passenger Pigeons
by Ken Rodgers

Given Enough Time:
Song Poems of Hugh Shacklett

Chapbooks by Jonah Raskin:
Letters of Love
Auras
Storm City

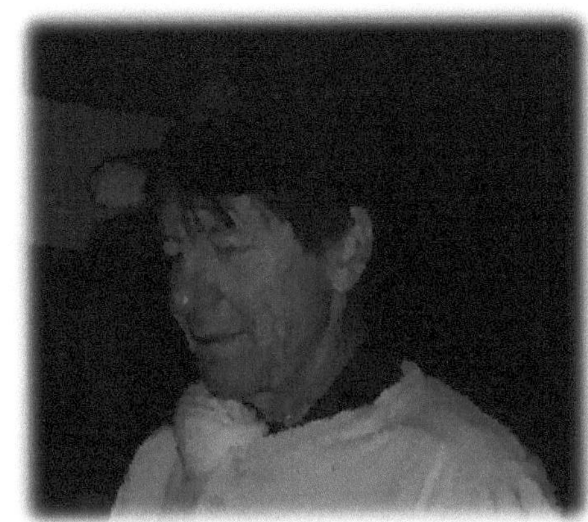

Music by Sarah Baker:

String Theories, CD
A live recording of the String Quartet written by Sarah Baker
for the International Virginia Woolf Conference, Person Theater, Sonoma
State University, 2002.

Dolly and the Lama Mountain Boys, CD
Recorded Live in Taos New Mexico.

By Timothy Williams
Figure on the Road
California Wildfires, Mountain Resorts, and a Lost Romantic Era

Baseball: In and Out of Time
A Rookie's Journey in the Senior Leagues

Gates of Wilbur
Narrative poetry from Colusa County, CA

Lunch at Lola's, Poetry Band's poetry and music CD

A Child's Christmas in Wales, a Voice Performance
written by Dylan Thomas, recorded by Jane Clark
at Jane Gets a Studio, Timothy Williams, and Susan Bono.

Endnotes

[i] Yeats, William, Butler. [i] *The Wanderings of Oisin—Book II*
Collected Poems of W.B. Yeats. Definitive Edition , New York. The Macmillan Company. 1956